WHO EATS WHAT?

DESERT
FOOD CHAINS

by Rebecca Pettiford

pogo

Ideas for Parents and Teachers

Pogo Books let children practice reading informational text while introducing them to nonfiction features such as headings, labels, sidebars, maps, and diagrams, as well as a table of contents, glossary, and index.

Carefully leveled text with a strong photo match offers early fluent readers the support they need to succeed.

Before Reading

- "Walk" through the book and point out the various nonfiction features. Ask the student what purpose each feature serves.
- Look at the glossary together. Read and discuss the words.

Read the Book

- Have the child read the book independently.
- Invite him or her to list questions that arise from reading.

After Reading

- Discuss the child's questions. Talk about how he or she might find answers to those questions.
- Prompt the child to think more. Ask: What other desert animals and plants do you know about? What food chains do you think they are a part of?

Pogo Books are published by Jump!
5357 Penn Avenue South
Minneapolis, MN 55419
www.jumplibrary.com

Library of Congress Cataloging-in-Publication Data

Pettiford, Rebecca, author.
  Desert food chains / by Rebecca Pettiford.
    pages cm. – (Who eats what?)
  Audience: Ages 7-10.
  Includes bibliographical references and index.
  ISBN 978-1-62031-301-5 (hardcover: alk. paper) –
  ISBN 978-1-62496-353-7 (ebook)
  1. Desert ecology–Juvenile literature. 2. Food chains (Ecology)–Juvenile literature. 3. Desert animals–Juvenile literature. I. Title.
  QH541.5.D4P48 2016
  577.54–dc23

                                                    2015022982

Series Editor: Jenny Fretland VanVoorst
Series Designer: Anna Peterson
Photo Researcher: Anna Peterson

Photo Credits: Alamy, 18-19; Bob Hermann, 20-21tm; Corbis, 12-13; Dreamstime, 20-21t; Getty, 3, 16, 17; National Geographic, 11; Science Source, 14-15, 20-21bm; Shutterstock, 1, 4, 5, 6-7, 10; SuperStock, cover, 8-9; Thinkstock, 20-21b, 23.

Printed in the United States of America at Corporate Graphics in North Mankato, Minnesota.

TABLE OF CONTENTS

CHAPTER 1
The Driest Place on Earth.....................4

CHAPTER 2
The Desert Food Chain 10

CHAPTER 3
Food Chain Close-Ups 16

ACTIVITIES & TOOLS
Try This!.............................. 22
Glossary 23
Index............................. 24
To Learn More......................... 24

CHAPTER 1

THE DRIEST PLACE ON EARTH

The desert is the driest **biome** on Earth. It gets less than 10 inches (25 centimeters) of rain each year.

Some desert soils are rocky. Others have a lot of sand. During the day, most deserts are hot. At night, they are cold.

The Arizona desert is hot and dry, but it is full of life. How do living things survive? They **adapt**.

Shrubs and trees have small leaves. This helps them save water.

A **cactus** stores water in its stem. Sharp **spines** protect it from hungry animals.

WHERE ARE THEY?

You can find deserts all over the world. The Sahara Desert is the largest. It covers 3.6 million square miles (9.4 million square kilometers). Antarctica is a cold desert. It is dry, and not many plants can grow there.

■ = Deserts

N
W—E
S

Most desert animals are active at night. During the day, they escape the heat by resting in **burrows** or in the shade of plants.

They do not need a lot of water. They get most of their water from plants.

burrow

CHAPTER 2

THE DESERT FOOD CHAIN

All living things need energy to survive. Plants create it from the sun, water, and soil. Animals get energy by eating.

A **food chain** describes what they eat. It shows how energy flows from plants to animals. Each link in the chain is fed by the one before it.

jackrabbit
(consumer)

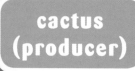

cactus
(producer)

Plants like cactuses are **producers**. They use energy from the sun, soil, and water to make their own food. They are the first link in the food chain.

Deer and jackrabbits eat plants. They are **consumers**, the next link in the chain.

DID YOU KNOW?

Why do jackrabbits have long ears? Their long ears let out heat to help them stay cool.

Snakes and eagles are **predators**. They eat consumers. Predators are next in the food chain.

Larger predators will also eat smaller predators. For example, a fox will eat a snake.

rattlesnake
(predator)

mouse
(consumer)

CHAPTER 3

....

FOOD CHAIN CLOSE-UPS

Let's look at a simple food chain.

Plants produce seeds. A kangaroo rat eats the seeds for energy.
A roadrunner eats the rat.

A coyote eats the roadrunner.
In time, the coyote dies.
What happens next?

When animals die, **decomposers** such as **vultures** and beetles break down the bodies. The nutrients from the dead matter pass into the soil. This helps plants grow.

turkey vulture (decomposer) ······▶

TAKE A LOOK!

. . . .

One desert food chain might look something like this:

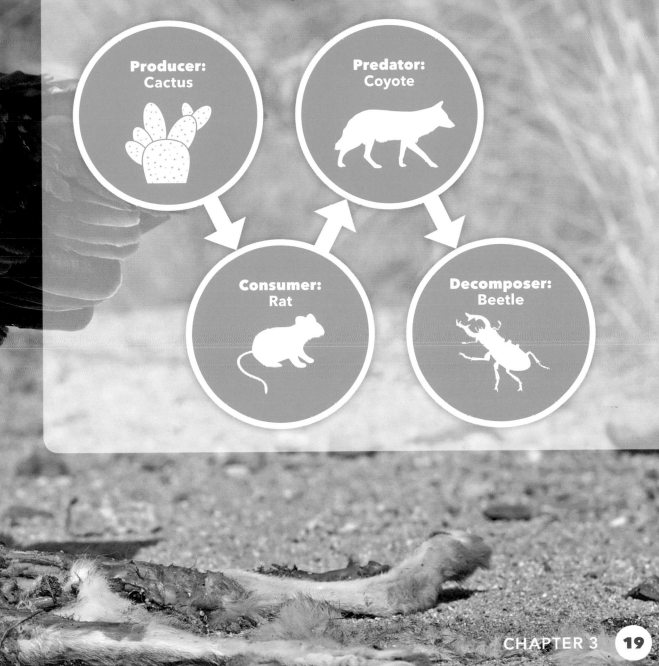

Let's look at another food chain.

1) A **cactus wren** eats cactus fruit.

2) A snake eats the wren.

3) A hawk eats the snake.

4) When the hawk dies, beetles break down its body. The nutrients return to the soil. They will help new plants grow.

The food chain continues!

DID YOU KNOW?

What happens if a type of plant or animal dies out? The food chain will change. For example, if insects disappear, desert toads will have nothing to eat. They will die, too.

ACTIVITIES & TOOLS

BREAKFAST FOOD CHAIN

No matter where you live, no matter what you eat, you are part of many food chains. Let's look at a few of them.

Think about what you had for breakfast. Try working backwards to create a food chain for your meal. Did you have eggs for breakfast? Trace the eggs back to the chicken, the chicken back to the grain, and the grain back to the sun. Did you have milk on your cereal? Trace the milk back to the cow, the cow back to the grass, and so on.

Draw a picture of your meal showing the different food chains that combined to create it. See if you can connect the various food chains. For example, the sun made the grass grow. Cows ate the grass and eventually gave you milk. But that same sun grew the grains that made your bread or that fed the chickens that laid the eggs you ate. It grew the trees that gave oranges for your orange juice. How many chains connected to make your breakfast?

GLOSSARY

adapt: Changing to better survive the conditions of a natural area.

biome: A large area on the earth defined by its weather, land, and the type of plants and animals that live there.

burrows: Holes or tunnels dug by small animals and used for shelter.

cactus: A leafless desert plant with a thick stem that usually has spines, bright flowers, and no leaves.

cactus wren: A type of bird that lives in the southwestern United States.

consumers: Animals that eat plants.

decomposers: Life forms that break down dead matter.

food chain: An ordering of plants and animals in which each uses or eats the one before it for energy.

predators: Animals that hunt and eat other animals.

producers: Plants that make their own food from the sun, soil, and water.

spines: Sharp points on a plant stem.

vultures: Large birds that feed on dead animals.

INDEX

animals 6, 8, 10, 11, 18, 20

Antarctica 7

biome 4

cactus 6, 8, 13, 20

climate 4, 5, 6

consumers 13, 14

day 5, 8

decomposers 18

energy 10, 11, 13, 16

locations 7

night 5, 8

nutrients 18, 20

plants 6, 7, 8, 10, 11, 13, 16, 18, 20

predators 14

producers 13

rain 4, 8

Sahara Desert 7

soil 5, 10, 13, 18, 20

sun 10, 13

water 6, 8, 13

TO LEARN MORE

Learning more is as easy as 1, 2, 3.

1) Go to www.factsurfer.com

2) Enter "desertfoodchains" into the search box.

3) Click the "Surf" to see a list of websites.

With factsurfer, finding more information is just a click away.